Following God into the Future

CONTENTS

Published by Christian Board of Publication, St. Louis, Missouri
Writer: Phillip E. Hoyle   Art Director: Michael A. Domínguez
Editor: Terry P. Rothermich   Cover design: Michael Foley
Series Editor: Michael E. Dixon   Interior design: Arista Graphics and Elizabeth Wright

FAITH CROSSINGS

WELCOME TO FOLLOWING GOD INTO THE FUTURE

IF...

you are saying "Help! I'm a leader! What do I do next?" go to pages 5–8.

you want to read a really neat article about using computers for Christian growth, go to page 9.

you want to schedule the leaders and locations for this study, turn to page 15.

you are getting ready for the first meeting of your FAITH CROSSINGS group and want to read Session 1 before you get there (always a good idea), it begins on page 16. Be certain to read the Introduction as well. It gives information on how to plan and structure the course.

you want to discover unique activities to wrap up your FAITH CROSSINGS experience, check out "Enriching the Experience" on page 76.

you want to find out more about the FAITH CROSSINGS series as a whole, see the information on page 78.

you have interest in reading through all of the scripture texts before beginning the course to get a sense of atmosphere or occasion, here they are:

Session 1: John 16:16–28

Session 2: Matthew 24:42–44

Session 3: Ecclesiastes 1; Revelation 21:5

Session 4: Deuteronomy 6:4–6, 20–25; Psalm 78:1–8

Session 5: Ezekiel 10, 12, 37

Session 6: Isaiah 60:1–5; 64:1–8

FOLLOWING GOD INTO THE FUTURE

AN INTRODUCTION

This course combines the themes of time and change. The *time* emphasis focuses on the future. The *changes* are realized in the future and are thus seen as its outcome. In the weeks your group meets, you will consider your personal lives, the life of your group, and the life of the church to which your group is connected. Through the readings, discussions, and activities you will explore how the themes affect your daily life and your interactions with the world. The considerations will enrich both your social life and your faith experiences. Activities will help you understand how you can more fully follow the leading of Jesus in your own time and into a changing future.

Time occurs. It is difficult to describe. Sometimes it can be measured, sometimes not. In this exploration we are more interested in *quality* measurements than in chronological. Thus, we will examine time through metaphor and symbol. Artist Corita Kent writes, "We don't really know what exists in the universe, so we have to be alert to see what we've not seen before. Look at something around you and say about whatever catches your eye, I don't understand that object now.

"We don't understand the fullness of everything, of anything. Things constantly change, and we may have seen an object only five minutes ago and thought we knew it—but now it is very different. To be able to adjust to these subtle differences means looking anew with what new materials we have gathered up inside ourselves—as well as noting what changes have taken place within the object. We need to be aware of what we don't yet know" (Jan Steward and Corita Kent, *Learning by Heart*, Bantam, New York, N.Y., 1992, p. 12).

Apply Corita's thoughts about "observation" as you work through this book about *time* and *change*. Although you will not be looking at an object to draw it, you will be considering these two concepts from varying points of view. Your own changes will affect what you believe, respond to, and learn. The perspectives of others in the group can open your own imagination to new possibilities. Open your eyes. Take a creative look at time—how it passes, how it breathes through existence, how it ebbs and flows from present to future, how it scripts your own life.

Making choices

The resources contained in this book are printed for six sessions of a group that meets for an hour and a half or longer. If you plan to use these resources in a church school class or other group that meets for an hour or less, you will want to make some decisions for each session. The simplest approach is to divide each of the six sessions into two plans. Each section ("Connecting with One Another," "Connecting with the Theme," etc.) contains more than one activity. Divide them up, choosing at least one activity from each main section. The only thing lacking will be the section called "Before the Session." Since there are other content-oriented articles elsewhere in each session, you can choose one of these as the lead article for your second session.

You may find it helpful to ask an individual or group of two or three people to divide the sessions at the outset of the course. List the titles of each activity for each of your sessions. Make copies of this list for each group member to place with his or her book.

IS IT MY TURN TO LEAD?

By Cathy Myers Wirt

Remember these leadership tips:

- ✓ **Read** the lesson more than once before leading it.
- ✓ Allow enough time to **gather materials or resources** you may need.
- ✓ **Pray** for the group members by name during the week.
- ✓ Create a **spirit of hospitality** and welcome in the meeting space through decoration, refreshments (if appropriate to your time), name tags if needed.
- ✓ Offer brief gathering times for quick **sharing of news** of the congregation/group.
- ✓ If sensitive topics arise, agree on a policy of **confidentiality.** Stories told in a group should be shared outside the group only when permission has been given.
- ✓ **Take all questions seriously** as a sign of the respect we hold for one another.
- ✓ If a person in the group has had a **tragedy** during the week, take time to deal with it, even if it means delaying the session.
- ✓ **Direct** persons with serious emotional or spiritual dilemmas to the pastor.
- ✓ **Call persons who are absent** from the group during the week to check in on them and let them know that they have been missed.
- ✓ Encourage group members to **invite new people** to the group.
- ✓ **Ask for help** when you come across a topic or a problem in a group. You don't have to do this alone!
- ✓ **Allow silence** in the group while people think. Don't jump in too quickly to fill the quiet.
- ✓ Start and end the group with a **time of prayer.**
- ✓ Begin and end the session **on time.**

- ✓ **Vary your leading style** between thoughtful discussion, activity, and visual/auditory experiences. People learn in different ways.
- ✓ Connect the life of the group to the **congregation and the wider church.**
- ✓ **Watch the news media** for examples of the topics you are studying and bring in the articles for discussion and prayer.
- ✓ **Thank God** for the learning you are enjoying by leading the group. Leadership is one of the best ways to learn and increase your own faith.
- ✓ **Don't assume** that the people in the room know each other well.
- ✓ **Don't argue.** When strongly different opinions are expressed, try to avoid a win/lose style of discussion.
- ✓ **Invite but don't coerce people to discuss.** Some people learn by listening and may be fully attentive without speaking.
- ✓ Help keep one person from **monopolizing the discussion.** Pass the discussion to another person by saying, "[name], what do you think about this idea/story?" Try always to do this in love.
- ✓ **Avoid getting sidetracked** by talking about people not in the room. Try to keep the discussion about the experiences and ideas of those in the room.
- ✓ **Avoid becoming unfocused** on the session. A group that has spun into other topics can be brought back by statements like "What in the session reminded you of that?" or "Wow, how did we get to this topic from today's lesson?" or "What you just said reminded me about our lesson today because…."

RACING THE CLOCK
A Leader's Guide to Getting through a Session

A typical FAITH CROSSINGS session gives more activities than time may allow. That's good news—there's a lot to choose from; and bad news—how do you choose? That depends. When you're leading a group of adults, there are a lot of variables! An activity that may take five minutes for one group may lead to a twenty-minute discussion in another. With all that in mind, here are some suggestions.

▲ Encourage everyone to read "Before the Session" before arriving. This section provides continuity and background to help the group members start "on the same page." Then the leader doesn't have to take time to summarize the information.

▲ In most cases, each session has four basic movements, each beginning with the phrase "Connecting with…" Be sure that you spend some time with each movement. (See the paragraph below on how to adapt this flow to a forty-five minute church school session.)

▲ Note the key activities. 🔑 This logo after the title of an activity is your clue that it is essential to the session. If you don't have enough time to cover everything, be sure you cover the key activities.

▲ Pick and choose from the remaining activities, according to your interests and the interests of the group. If your group doesn't like an arts-based activity, for example, that may be a good one to draw a big X through before the session even begins.

▲ Go with the flow. Don't let agenda anxiety put a premature end to a really great discussion. And don't drag out an activity that people aren't responding to—just summarize and move on.

Adapting to a church school setting

Each session is written for a ninety-minute group setting. If you want to use it in church school, how do you adapt? Two suggestions:

1. Allow twelve weeks for the six sessions. During the first week of a given session, cover what you can and close with a prayer. When the next week's session begins, summarize what the group covered the first week. Then work through the remaining activities.

2. Lead one session a week for six weeks. If you do this, there will probably be time for little more than the key activities. Highlight some of the important discussion questions you wish to include from the other activities. Encourage the group members to read the whole session, but select those activities for group use that connect to your particular group.

CYBERLEARNING— COMPUTERS, INTERNET, AND THE GROUP

By Kenneth R. Watson

The presence of one or more computers in the educational setting, even in congregations, is becoming a fact of life. Church educators are beginning to understand how computers can be used effectively, and they are becoming sensitive to the promises and problems of this technology. When used skillfully, emerging computer technology can be a powerful enhancement to the educational mission. On the other hand, if we misunderstand the role of computers, they can become distractions and disruptions, wasting valuable resources.

Variety of Uses

Among the many ways in which computers can be integrated into a curriculum, three approaches seem to dominate: (1) as the primary source of instructional materials and activities, (2) as providers of supplementary resources to a more traditional curriculum, or (3) as tools in the implementation of projects. Each of these tasks has its unique assets and liabilities.

There was a time, early in the development of computerized instruction, when we assumed (or feared) that computers would take over the task of content delivery. The information resources that a computer could tap and its ability to patiently adjust to the learner's needs seemed to be almost limitless. As we mature in our use of the computer, we begin to understand that there are serious limitations to how much of the educational task can be replaced by computer-student interaction. However, there are times when the special capabilities of computers make them well suited to the task of providing primary content. When an individual wants to explore a topic like the history of Jerusalem, there are excellent resources now available that can take the learner through the material in ways that are almost impossible with printed resources. With very little leader intervention, the learner can explore and direct the learning experience to match her or his personal style. Just as videotapes are often used as the basis for a classroom experience, so multimedia computer technology can be used to guide individuals or groups through a variety of subjects.

Supplementing an already existing curriculum is probably the most common use of current computer technology. When an elementary-age class studies the life of King David, they can turn to the computer for activities and resources to enhance the classroom instruction. A variety of programs provide engaging narrative and practice tasks that help the learner understand and remember the content and issues of the life of David. In addition, learners can explore the growing number of encyclopedia-format resources to do their own research for incorporation into the classroom setting. As a motivational tool and as a repository of information, computers add effectively to the learning experience.

Computers can be useful in a variety of activities not directly associated with content delivery. A junior high class can put together a calendar, using original artwork, for sale as a fund-raising project. A group of older youth can publish a youth newsletter with powerful but inexpensive desktop publishing software. Young children can exercise their creative talents in art or music or writing, assisted by the computer, and publish the amazing results, to the delight of family and friends. The possibilities for projects and activities are limitless.

The Emergence of the Internet

If we examine the material written just ten years ago about how computers might be used effectively in the church, we are struck by how little attention was paid to the possibilities of computers as communication resources. We could not imagine the pervasive presence of the Internet and the World Wide Web. Yet today we could not think of computers in the church without serious attention to how this new fact of life provides opportunities, and perils, for our educational ministries.

An obvious use of the Internet today is as a research tool of boundless scope. A junior high class studying the stewardship of money and talents can explore the impact of vocational decisions by accessing the vast data on cost-of-living and employment opportunities in various parts of the world. An older elementary class can search the Web for information about Pentecost and learn how it is celebrated in several different traditions. Adults interested in the quality of nonprofit outreach organizations can explore how well specific groups are doing, with assistance from umbrella and watchdog groups that provide this type of information "online." Such research is common, even in elementary schools today, and adds an interesting and challenging element to our kit of teaching methods and tools.

At least as common as accessing the Web for information is the increasing use of the Internet for communicating individually and as groups. This presents us with enormous capabilities unavailable to previous generations. Computer pen pals are a common experience for children today, hooking up with their peers in other communities to share information or work on cooperative projects. Hundreds of thousands of special interest groups exist on the Internet, where topics are broadly and passionately discussed. Geography has almost ceased to be relevant in getting people together for dialogue or joint action. A church school class in rural Missouri can link with another group in Australia. A missionary in the Philippines can provide live reports to partner churches in the United States. Even video links, still somewhat limited in quality, are becoming quite common on the Internet with rather inexpensive equipment.

With a minimum of work, sites can be found throughout the World Wide Web that provide on-line activities for children. Some of those sites are religious in nature and offer some exciting possibilities for outreach ministries that are not limited by the geographic bounds of parishes. There are sites that provide Bible-learning activities, religious theme explorations geared to children, devotional resources, and youth programming ideas. Anyone with minimal skills in searching the Web can turn up dozens of interesting and high-quality sites providing resources for use on Sunday mornings or in youth fellowships. They could also be used to give parents and children guidance in choosing quality places to access from home. Even allowing for the adage that ninety percent of what is on the Web is junk or worse, the vast numbers of resources included in that remaining ten percent are excellent tools in the educational repertoire.

Guidelines and Caveats

Every tool or technique comes with a set of cautions and limitations. That is especially true of new and developing resources like computers. Listed here, in no particular order of importance, are some issues needing attention by anyone seeking to use this technology in Christian education.

Fragmentation and depersonalization. A frequently heard concern of both the experienced and the inexperienced computer user is whether this technology will continue, or even accelerate, the trend toward isolating individuals in front of a TV screen or monitor, rather than providing healthy interpersonal interaction. The concern is as real with the use of computers in education as it is in many other aspects of modern living. Most educators and parents would decry the use of any tool that drove people apart rather than bringing them together. However, as in many other such debates, the issue can be addressed effectively with a little forethought. One church I know of has a standing rule that computer activities at the church will nearly always be done in a cooperative learning style: a minimum of two learners per computer who work together toward a carefully defined goal. This rule is enforced even when there are sufficient computers available for each learner. Even creative art and music tasks can be done this way. Making sure that church school teachers are actively involved with each learner while he or she works on a computer activity is an important guideline to keep the learner from becoming isolated from the community of faith.

Safety. This issue has been a hot-button topic for many discussions involving the use of the World Wide Web with children. While many children are learning rules for appropriate on-line dialogue (e.g., what information should or should not be divulged to on-line strangers), the need for vigilance remains. It is not as easy to access highly inappropriate material accidentally as anecdotes would have us believe. However, it is possible. Children should not be on-line without adequate supervision by someone who knows at a glance what is happening. Chat rooms and interactive Web pages are becoming so common and so familiar to children that oversight is a necessity. Never depend on software protection programs to do the job of a responsible adult. Most children and youth learn very quickly how to bypass or subvert the most sophisticated security blockers on Web browsers.

Quality. Caring and concerned educators would seldom adopt or use a curriculum resource without attending to the quality of the material. In the early days of personal computer software, available programs were dull, artless experiences. Even today, with all the bells and whistles of multimedia programming, there is enormous variation in the visual and educational quality of materials. Activities unappealing to the senses will not hold learners who are used to high-quality secular materials. Even good content, wrapped in an unattractive presentation, will often be dismissed in favor of shallow material presented in an engaging format. Do not depend on the software publisher's ads. If you are inexperienced, ask others who are knowledgeable educators with experience in software to look at it with you. Field test it with your learners and share their reactions and your evaluations with others. Most software, once purchased and installed, cannot be returned. Wise stewardship of our resources would have us move carefully when selecting either equipment or software.

Theological stance. This may be the most often overlooked or ignored issue when dealing with computer learning and activities. We are often so happy to find material on the topic we want, or the visual impact is so outstanding, that we incorporate it into our curriculum without appropriate consideration or analysis. Bible games that include violence as an integral part of the learning activity, retelling biblical stories with highly questionable moralizing and applications, and Web pages that are full of objectionable proselytizing or theologically offensive content are just a few examples of why careful review and selection are so critical. *Never select material on the basis of look or topic without attending to its substantive content.*

The power of the new computer and communications technologies is awesome. They provide us with rich resources and wonderful new techniques and opportunities. We need to lay claim to them just as we have the typewriter, the tape recorder, the filmstrip projector, the VCR, and (for many) the DVD. But we must always be aware that this technology comes with a message. Content and the technology are interwoven. Our task is to appraise and implement it with appropriate attention to educational and theological evaluation.

Kenneth R. Watson is Associate Minister at First Christian Church in Columbia, Missouri, and a specialist in computer education.

WHEN FAITH CROSSINGS HAPPEN

Our life experiences and our faith often cross paths. We come to moments when we need our faith to help us interpret the meaning of our life experiences and to make Christian choices. Or our life experiences cause us to rethink our beliefs. When we come to such crossing points between faith and daily life, our lives change.

 Faith crossings happen when people share their beliefs lovingly and honestly, in a context of faith and love. The way other people live out and express their faith shapes our own. A Christian, small group setting creates a context for this to happen. We become pilgrims together on a faith journey. Every FAITH CROSSINGS session promotes this interaction with activities under this heading and icon: **Connecting with one another.**

 Faith crossings happen when we open ourselves to new discoveries about life and faith. Whether it's in reading the Bible or the daily news, downloading from the Internet or watching television, we receive new information that helps shape our understanding. Every FAITH CROSSINGS session promotes new learning with activities under this heading and icon: **Connecting with the theme.**

 Faith crossings happen when we decide what to do next. How do our faith and experiences lead us to change the course of our daily lives? Toward what actions do our faith crossings prod us? Every FAITH CROSSINGS session promotes this decision making with activities under this heading and icon: **Connecting with life.**

 Faith crossings happen when we celebrate God's presence in our midst. God calls us to respond, to praise, to pray, to worship, to love. Every FAITH CROSSINGS session promotes worship and reflection with activities under this heading and icon: **Connecting with God.**

SESSION SCHEDULE

Session 1
When _____Leader_____
Where_____

Session 2
When _____Leader_____
Where_____

Session 3
When _____Leader_____
Where_____

Session 4
When _____Leader_____
Where_____

Session 5
When _____Leader_____
Where_____

Session 6
When _____Leader_____
Where_____

Special Activities
When _____Leader_____
Where_____

1

Millennium Mania

Session Focus: The changing of the millennium brings with it a great deal of commercial hype and religious excitement. It can help us focus our hopes and fears about the future and raise issues about how we perceive time. These ideas affect the way we live as disciples.

Scripture Used: John 16:16–28

BEFORE THE SESSION

Read and reflect on this meditation.

The approaching millennium has brought on a mania of time consciousness that embraces popular entertainment, greedy promotion, and thoughtful reflection. Television scripts and titles exploit the word. Companies advertise products to help buyers enter both the new century and millennium successfully. Educators, therapists, and philosophers integrate the concept into current professional theories. Whole-life networks publish and advertise their work using images of the millennium. Countless religious movements preach the end of one age and the onset of a new order. Denominations have even organized and sustained themselves throughout the twentieth century on the basis of millennial anticipation.

Millennium is an age-old Christian theme renewed to a position of prominence in the past two and a half centuries. Several social concerns and spiritual concepts complement its reemergence. Fears related to ecological crises heighten the anticipation of change and the alarm of devastation. Some New Age doctrines support visions of calamitous or long-overdue change heralded by astrological convergences. The stress surrounding modern medicine's seeming inability to speedily contain viral diseases fuels anxiety. The theme embraces new interpretations and surprising supporters.

The variety of Christian beliefs about the direction and end of history might amaze us. Christians in the first century anticipated the end of the age. Some thought it would happen with the destruction of the Jerusalem temple in 70 C.E. Others waited for the end to take place in a less immediate future. Their belief compelled many of these early Christians to forsake worldly wealth and interests. They wanted to dedicate their lives to what they determined was God's work.

Throughout Christian history, when times have become difficult, some preacher or another has begun to harp on the theme of the imminent return of Christ and the end of the world. Their ideas have been interpreted differently and have served a variety of purposes. Sometimes the preaching has helped reform the personal ethics of individuals. The words of judgment have also been used to encourage governments to be more just. Some leaders have taught the images as spiritual ideas that relate to an individual's life or a society's ability to survive. The teachings of the end of the age are usually interpreted as both symbolic and literal events to encourage grace in the human community and to threaten the end if no reforms can be readily realized.

Millennial Glossary

Review these words and keep them at hand for the discussions in this and coming chapters.

▲ *Millennium*—a period of 1,000 years in Western calendar keeping; in Revelation 20 a symbol of a long time under Christ's reign; a long period of good government or of happiness.

▲ *Eschatology*—a theological term for the consideration of the end times; arises from the preaching of biblical prophets of the end of an age or the end of time itself.

1. Discuss the future 🔑

What hopes and fears do you have about the future? the future of your family? friends? church? community? What main factors in your life cause you to think hopefully? What idea most discourages you? What person has contributed most to your ability to hope? to fear?

What kinds of things do you save money for? What relationship between the desire and the ability to save do you observe? What are you saving for right now? How do savings interpret your hopes for the future? How do savings promise to help fulfill your hopes? What stands in the way of the fulfillment of these hopes? Who shares your hopes?

2. Pray for one another

Relate individual experiences of endings and beginnings that are part of your week. Ask questions only to clarify issues and prayer requests. Avoid discussing the issues. Offer the things for which you want prayers and remembrances.

You may choose to pray a simple prayer of intercession right now or perhaps at the end of the session. If your group meets for over an hour, take time now to pray together. If not, do this early in the session so prayer requests flavor the discussion. At the session's end, pray together about class experiences and issues.

3. Clarify your concerns

Some Christian thinkers are not at all concerned about the end of an age. Quite a few, in fact, believe that the biblical symbols of the new age have already been fulfilled. Others argue that preoccupation with these ancient symbols is out of date or represents a misunderstanding of the intent of the language of those early days. New ideas of eschatology, both symbolic and literal, have become important in twentieth-century theology.

CONNECTING WITH ONE ANOTHER

For Activity 1, gather in a circle so you can see one another as you talk together. Use these questions to open the session. If you are planning two sessions, consider using one paragraph for the first and the other for the subsequent gathering.

Examine several understandings of the idea of the end of time or the end of the world. Decide which perspectives most appeal to you.

Christians in the late twentieth century are alert to a second kind of eschatological possibility. The creation and application of nuclear weapons make human destruction of the world not only possible, but a genuine threat. The end of the world due to a national miscalculation or even a technological breakdown makes war seem an impossibility to the future of human community. If we can destroy the world and ourselves, we had better find ways to prevent the kind of disaster an all-out nuclear war promises to bring.

A third kind of eschatological sensitivity captures the imaginations of some contemporary theologians. Not only has humanity created the possibility of destroying the world with warfare, but it has also actualized significant ecological devastation. Current ideas of the end often incorporate the destruction of land, water, air, and species through various kinds of human-produced pollution, mismanagement, or greed. Whatever the particular view, Christians seem excruciatingly aware of new possibilities of an end to the world. It is small wonder that these perceptions create ample anxiety in our time.

4. A 1,000-year-old event

What happens when humanity enters a new century or a new millennium? We have written records to provide some insights. Author Richard Erdoes describes life in Europe in the century prior to the year 1000. Many signs and portents frightened the common folk. They quoted scriptures in support of their anticipation of the Last Judgment and the destruction of the earth. Richard Erdoes describes an emotional midnight mass held at St. Peter's Basilica in Rome, December 31, 999. Some people were so worked up they fainted, and a few died.

> But when the fatal hour passed and the earth did not open to swallow up church and worshipers, and when no fire fell from heaven burning everything alive into ashes, all stirred as

CONNECTING WITH THE THEME

Read and discuss this historical account and any comparisons or questions you have in light of observations today in the group.

if awakening from a bad dream. Then everybody breathed a great sigh of relief amid much weeping and laughing. Husband and wife, servant and master embraced and even unreconciled enemies hailed each other as friends and exchanged the kiss of peace. Then all the bells of St. Peter's, of the Lateran, of the Aventine, of every church upon the Seven Hills of Rome, began to ring, praising the Lord as with one single voice. The bitter cup had passed, the world was like reborn and all humankind rejoiced, as related by many ancient chroniclers" (Richard Erdoes, *A.D. 1000: Living on the Brink of Apocalypse*, Harper & Row, 1988, pp. 8–9).

Then, as at times before and since, people gathered for worship wearing special garments and waited for the end, or some other cataclysmic event.

5. Gain a biblical understanding 🔑

The Bible embraces at least three contrasting notions of time: cyclical time, chronological time, and crisis-related time. These are not biblical concepts per se but types of time perception on which various passages are based. The perspectives are implicit in the texts. One can see in some texts the idea that things happen over and over *(cyclical time)* and in others the idea that new things are being created *(chronological time)*.

Probably *cyclical time* is the most ancient in that its origin is based in agriculture. Seasons change, and the best time for planting is remembered by the community. The moon's cycles, matched to human fertility, become a predictable measure for time. The repetition of planting and harvest, of the seasons, of the human lifetime, create a cyclic understanding of time. Cyclical time is particularly important in

Three groups can plan and read a brief sketch or pantomime interpreting the three kinds of time mentioned here.

Genesis, in Judges, and in much of the poetry of the Old Testament.

Chronological time is implied in passages such as Psalm 90:10, in which the writer recognizes that a human may expect to live to age 70. Another chronological measure was the "generation" (e.g., "from one generation to another"), though this might be considered genealogical time by some. Chronological expectations were common to both Testaments. The wisdom literature of the Old Testament suggests people should become aware of the passing of time so as not to misuse the opportunities it affords.

Job, Proverbs, and Ecclesiastes

The apostle Paul urges readers to value chronological time and to see in it another perspective of time.

Romans 5:6 and Galatians 4:4

In Paul's theology, God's time was *crisis-related* time (Greek *kairos*). The crisis can be seen in Paul's images of the revelation of a mystery—God's time and timeline relating natural and human events to God's purposes. Perhaps one can say that the most important things happen when "the time is right" from God's perspective. We Christians live in a balanced state. Our earthly existence discovers its importance as a crisis of realizing and fulfilling God's purpose(s). When God acts in human history, in church life, and in individual experience, new worlds of possibility result.

6. Consider a modern time synthesis

As a group, read and discuss this perception of time.

Another meaningful consideration of time for our day can be called *developmental time*. With a focus on change, this perspective combines the cyclical time idea with the idea of stages of development throughout the chronological experience of a person. Developmental time incorporates crisis time in the idea that one passes through various crises of understanding and behavior at predictable times in one's life. In a corporate or natural context, the development can be much larger in scope. This perspective sees both the "inevitable" and "accidental," processes important to outcome development. The combining of perspectives has been most influential in the natural sciences, psychology, history, and education. One can mark time in relationship with expectations of development and change.

7. Discover time concepts

Jesus anticipated the end of his time with his disciples. In John's Gospel, Jesus addresses his disciples at their final supper together. The disciples have difficulty grasping his message (though in this Gospel Jesus talks five times about his going away). Read the speech (John 16:16–28) using one person (or several) to read Jesus' words, another to be the narrator, and the rest to be the disciples. Listen for indications of time, its effect, and its importance for the future. Invite participants to choose a favorite or especially meaningful verse from this text as it is dialogued.

8. Discuss endings

What ideas did you pick up about time in reading the passage in John? What kinds of futures might Jesus have hinted at in the speech? How does the assumption that he was talking about next week contrast with the assumption that he was talking about life beyond time? What other possibilities could afford rich readings of the text?

How do you think early disciples read this scripture? What possibilities can you imagine? What kind of hope did they find in it? How did it help them meet the crises of their lives? How did the text bring calm, peace, hope, or motivation to an early group of followers? How does the passage impress you? How does it help you? How might you summarize the time possibilities it opens for your life, the group, or the church?

Mark these in the text or list them on a flip chart or large sheets of paper (e.g., newsprint).

Circle the verse numbers or make note some way. This will be used under "Think about a scripture" (see p. 24).

Use these questions to discuss the passages you marked or listed in John (see Activity 7).

Following God into the Future

9. Summarize your interests

The nearness of a millennial change raises for many people perplexing issues about how humans perceive and mark time. Scythian monk Dionysius Exiguus, "the Little," miscalculated the date of Jesus' birth in the very calendar that became the norm for Western civilization. Jesus was born approximately six years before the first "Year of Our Lord." With such suspect time marking, we could ask just when will or did this third Christian millennium begin? Several years ago? If our calendar inaccurately indicates the change of time, why would we be anxious about it or even take note? In a world of cultural relativity, what does it say about us if we anticipate tremendous changes on the basis of a possibly inaccurate calendar?

If concern about the symbolic importance of a millennium cannot be accurately calculated by a calendar (e.g., does it begin in 2000 or 2001?), how is this symbol meaningful at all?

10. Make a calendar

Represent your concerns related to time through making a specialized calendar for your group's life and values.

As a group, plan and make a calendar to mark your time and interpret your lives. Begin with a basic list of group needs a calendar could meet (e.g., Zodiac signs, birthdays of friends, spaces for appointments and deadlines, concerts, holidays, celebrations). Will it include favorite quotes? Will it have other religions' significant liturgical dates? How can you represent crises, developmental time issues, and chronological occurrences? What holidays and special events will your calendar list? Will it include birthdays of group members? Will it include birth signs, phases of the moon and planets, natural occurrences, and such? What other considerations can ensure that the calendar is tailored to your group's needs? What materials will producing it require? When will you make it? Where will it be displayed?

11. Discuss the end

How does the image of the end of the world affect you? What kinds of images does the suggestion elicit? What are your favorite and not-so-favorite memories of such images (from readings, movies, videos, media)? What historical happenings (e.g., wars, natural disasters, environmental threats, changes in governments, new leaderships, emerging ideologies) help you imagine a major change in the world and in society? What do you see as some differences between "major change" and "the end"?

12. Think about a scripture

Ask any group member to read his or her favorite verse(s) from the scripture passage. Following the reading(s), and during a brief silence, think about the meanings for you. Close with this prayer litany:

CONNECTING WITH GOD

John 16:16–28

Say this as a leader-group litany or as a Group 1-Group 2 litany.

(1) This day to me, God, do thou bless,
(2) This very night, God, blessing give,
(1) Thou God of grace, O do thou bless
(2) All days and all the times I live;
(1) Thou God of grace, O do thou bless
(2) All days and all the times I live.
(1) God bless the path I walk above,
(2) God, bless the earth beneath my toes;
(1) God, bless me, give to me thy love,
(2) O God of gods, bless rest, repose;
(1) God, bless me, give to me thy love,
(2) O God of gods, bless my repose.

(*6 Benbecula—Praying with the Celts*, selected by G.R.D. McLean, William B. Eerdmans Publishing Company, 1996, p. 35.)

13. Close with prayer

See "Pray for one another," p. 18.

Invite anyone in the group to offer a prayer response to your time together or to pray for the items of intercession you named early in the session.

Following God into the Future

NOTES

2

The Bible: A Road Map or Crystal Ball?

Session Focus: Many people find in the Bible clear signs of the impending end of the world. If they are wrong, does it mean the Bible is wrong? What were the biblical writers trying to say in their time, and what can we learn from them for our time?

Scripture Used: Matthew 24:42–44

BEFORE THE SESSION

Underline or otherwise mark the sentences, phrases, or ideas that spark your imagination. Refer to them in the group discussion.

Discussions about religion often defy rational explanation. For instance, 28-year-old Jay talked about his family—his parents, who took the kids to church, his admiration for a minister, his involvement in a youth group, some conversions, his brother's ministry. He said he had faith and believed many things. He was not so sure about the way the Bible had been interpreted over the years, but he had special interest in the book of Revelation. Like many people, Jay had quit going to church, given up on the religious establishment, and become disillusioned with the ways the church judged his life. However, he remained intrigued with the book of Revelation. Was it fear? the allure of the future? the exotic aspect of symbolic knowledge?

Jay is not alone in his interest. Prophetic writings such as those found in the books of Daniel and

Revelation are only one type among several types of prophecy present in the Bible. Still, the type it represents is by far the most popular and challenging. Periodically, congregations ask their minister(s) to teach and preach from these apocalyptic writings. We seem hopeful to discover a secret answer to the future—kind of like reading tea leaves, cards, or palms.

Many people find in Daniel and Revelation clear signs of the impending end of the world. This begs the question, "When will these calamitous events take place?" Some readers find in such texts clear answers to the questions. More do not. If the folks who believe that these books indicate the imminent end of the world are correct, what about those who do not seem to care for such speculation? If the former are wrong, does it mean the Bible is wrong? While such simple questions to such complex issues can be misleading, they raise an important consideration. How are we to think about biblical meaning and helpfulness in times of great uncertainty and speculation?

Early Christians Believed

Refer to 1 Corinthians 15.

Apocalyptic assumptions were undoubtedly an important part of early Christian thinking, stemming, in large part, from belief in the resurrection of Jesus. Jesus was the first of many who would be raised from the dead. Early Christians lived in the hope that they, likewise, would be raised. The apostle Paul taught that the resurrection was central to the good news. For him, if the resurrection of the dead was untrue, there would be no reason to be in conflict with the synagogue or the state. There would also be no reason to suffer persecution and rejection. Paul clearly looked toward a "time beyond time," an existence in another (spiritual) realm in which the costs of living faithfully in this life would be made worthwhile. He focused on the resurrection of Christ as the main symbol of such a future.

The apocalyptic style of thinking made condemnation of various enemies sensible, placing current conflicts of the life of faith in a context of "spiritual warfare"—fighting a battle in heavenly places. This battle reflected itself in the troubles the Christians were facing. The forces of evil were posed against the forces of righteousness. Prophets predicted good would prevail. This interpretation of the worlds of heaven and earth gave (and still gives some) believers hope, enhancing the possibilities of hanging onto dreams and hopes in troubled times. In 1 Corinthians, Paul wrote that faithful believers would be caught up into this spiritually victorious world of heaven at the end of time.

Glossary of the Apocalypse

Learn these definitions and refer to them in discussion.

- ▲ *Apocalypse*—a prophetic writing that announces an upheaval in which evil spiritual forces are destroyed; Daniel and Revelation are such writings in the Bible.

- ▲ *Return of Christ*—anticipation of the early church in which Christ was to return to earth as judge of the living and the dead; the idea was related to images of the ascension and, later, in comparison with Jesus' birth (the first coming).

- ▲ *Day of the Lord*—any moment or time in which God's gift of judgment is fulfilled; its origins are in Old Testament prophecy and continue in the New Testament expectation of Jesus' return.

1. Talk and pray about present life issues 🔑

Describe some anxieties group members feel about the immediate future—in their lives, in the church, in the group, in the world. Are some experiencing or anticipating job changes? What are the worries of others whose children or family members

CONNECTING WITH ONE ANOTHER

Identify life issues relating to the immediate future.

Following God into the Future

recently moved (or will soon move) away from home? If any anticipate major changes due to birth, adoption, marriage, or divorce, what are the feelings about it? What kinds of concerns are present regarding health (either personal or someone else's)? What are the alternative visions about the future of your congregation or this group that participants might see? Use these concerns as prayer requests for intercession. Avoid discussing the ideas and pray about the requests as spoken.

2. Set the stage

Examine a variety of modern theological thoughts related to apocalypse.

Contemporary Christians subscribe to a variety of ideas about the future. Some expect the world to come to an end very soon and adroitly quote biblical signs of the times to prove their point. Others avoid the issue entirely. There are those who believe the end predicted in the Bible has already taken place. They reason that the prophets failed to anticipate the long extension of the church age or that the attempt to make literal their predictions misses the point that life was changed, that the world the church grew in was, in fact, a changed place and experience.

In terms of faith, questions about the spiritual view of apocalyptic writing are far more important than the consideration of time itself. We gain more from the Bible by asking how the view of spiritual warfare and conflict is helpful or unhelpful in our lives rather than focusing on the specific question of whether the Bible can tell us when things will happen.

See Luke 12:54–56 and Acts 1:7.

Jesus' teachings are an important guide to our thinking. Although he viewed the world in apocalyptic terms, he devalued speculation on the timeline of such occurrences. He was connected to the heavenly realm and fought a good fight on earth. He was faithful to his heavenly vision, praying constantly. He understood himself to be in conflict with the forces of evil, and he prophesied the destruction of the

Born in North Africa of Latin heritage, Augustine of Hippo (354–430) is renowned by many as the major figure in Christian thought and philosophy after the apostle Paul.

CONNECTING WITH THE THEME

Respond to this real-life situation. Ask an individual to read it to the group and then discuss your responses.

Jerusalem temple in apocalyptic fashion. Still, he advised his listeners not to conjecture about time but, rather, to do what they understood to be God's will.

Sometimes we might find ourselves reluctantly asking, "Is the Bible wrong?" For example, the imminent end of the world anticipated by New Testament writers has not yet come. Though two thousand years is a long time for *us*, perhaps it is not for God. There are a wealth of perspectives about the Bible and its teachings to discover. St. Augustine recommended most passages be interpreted with at least ten different approaches.

No matter what our personal theology, we all benefit from discovering various ways to interpret the Bible. One easy way to begin comprehending this is to gather numerous Bibles in different translations, find a familiar passage, and go around the group, each person reading a translation of the passage. Unfulfilled expectations can lead us into new riches of understanding as we open our imaginations and spirits.

3. Decide who was wrong

"My father believed that Christ would return in his lifetime. He understood the return as a symbol of hope—hope for humanity in the face of many changes that threatened his most cherished values. Dad was generous, always sharing what he had with others, tithing to his local congregation, supporting missions of various sorts, and eventually pastoring a congregation. He lived his life as a disciple of Jesus, taking his master's teachings seriously and often literally. He lived a meaningful and helpful life, but he was wrong about Jesus' return. At age 78, Dad died, but the event he had believed in and so longed for did not take place, at least not in the terms in which my father imagined it would occur."

Use these questions
to stimulate your
discussion.

Imagine you are talking with "Dad's" grandchildren. They ask you if Grandpa was wrong. What kinds of answers could you offer to their question? What can it mean to be right or wrong about a biblical understanding? How do our mistakes of interpretation benefit us? How might our more correct notions, as we perceive them, hurt us? How do happenings in our lives make a difference in the way we think?

Subdivide the group
for a simple Bible
study activity.
Provide each group
with blank paper
and a marker to
help members
present ideas.

4. Discover varied ideas within your group

In office break rooms, teachers' lounges, cafeterias, buses, bridge parties, and the like, you could find yourself talking about religion or the Bible with someone whose views differ greatly from yours. Perhaps they anticipate you will have beliefs just like theirs and are surprised when you do not. They may expect you to defend or explain your ideas in ways you are not interested in or cannot. Even within your class or subgroup there exist different opinions, viewpoints, and values. Learning about these differences can be instructive in clarifying your personal interests and ideas.

In groups of three or four, read aloud Matthew 24:42–44 and write down a few ideas generated by this text from each of the following perspectives:

- ▲ sociological (group life of the early church)

- ▲ historical (what was happening in the world at the time)

- ▲ a parable (a teaching form)

- ▲ an instruction guideline

- ▲ a meditation

- ▲ a revolutionary statement or principle

Write down the subgroups' ideas quickly. What are the favorite responses? Discuss what it means to have differing insights and ideas related to scripture.

5. Revisit the old

Use your imaginations and memories for this discussion.

From your conversation about Matthew 24:42–44 and other things you remember from the Bible, discuss ideas relating to the Bible's "purpose," both in ancient days and in our own time. What do you think Bible writers who predicted the end of the world or the end of an order were trying to say to their time? What value can biblical thought about the end of time have today? How is God active in the ideas? How does a backdrop of spirit-realm activity help one, or a group of people, with unexpected returns, unanticipated judgments, or unforeseen catastrophes?

Perhaps you have seen the movie "Apocalypse Now." What made the movie apocalyptic? The destruction, devastation, and conflict in Vietnam was a reflection of a larger, more powerful, and more influential "conflict of state." We notice an analogy. What influencing powers within "conflicts" and "endings" cause us to participate in destruction, war, and abuses? How can we define "spiritual" when we embrace the warfare or conflict metaphor? What is helpful or not with this metaphor? What other apocalyptic metaphors can you imagine?

6. Discuss discussions

CONNECTING WITH LIFE

Talk about this quote in light of different understandings and assumptions about the Bible and the end of time.

When we give names to things, we often assume that everything that goes by that name is alike (Jan Steward and Corita Kent, p. 21).

Discussions often leave people wondering about one another, especially when the discussions focus on religion, politics, or values. We categorize one another on one topic and let the name we affix (e.g., conservative, liberal, fundamentalist, radical, strange, off-the-wall) represent much more than is warranted. If our discussions go on long enough, we may be

Following God into the Future

surprised by the wonderful way in which other people's thoughts help them. We discover that other people are interesting and their perspectives are helpful. On the other hand, we may find ourselves rejected because we are too "something or other." Even more interesting, we could find ourselves shying away from discussions because we dislike being labeled or rejected for something we do not believe. How does such a point make communication difficult?

7. Discuss possibilities for transformation 🗝

List ideas about how the Bible can assist in spiritual transformation.

Remember to write down all the suggestions.

We need to ask open, helpful questions of the Bible and then expect to be transformed. What possibilities can your group brainstorm that describe kinds of transformation your reading of the Bible can bring? Avoid examining or discussing them until the group has listed a predetermined number of ideas (go for 25) or you simply run out of ideas. Take a group poll to get consensus of the 8–10 most helpful, then discuss those. Listen to and learn from one another. How do the ideas function as values? What do the values suggest? Try to summarize the group's ideas.

Discuss ways the Bible has been helpful in life situations.

Delineate how the Bible's ideas and the process of reading the Bible itself or hearing the Bible read, preached, or taught has helped in your life. How has it helped in dealing with personal crises (e.g., death of a loved one, loss of a job, threat to freedoms) and constructing visionary perceptions of the world? If it has not, why not? Summarize the experiences and values related to these uses of the Bible.

8. Construct a group theology of *difference* 🗝

As a group, write statements that interpret the value of *difference*.

Begin constructing a theology embracing differing emphases in the life of God and our common life. In small groups, write affirmations that embrace some kind of theological diversity. For example, you could affirm the diversity in contrasting religious faiths, among churches in your community, among members in your congregation, or even among individuals in the group. Another approach would be to contrast the changes in your own thought. Use the form "I used to believe...but now I believe...." Affirm your own diversity. Share the statements with the whole group and discuss how they help us grow in understanding our own religious experiences and ourselves.

9. Reflect on a poem

Lord, you called to me,
And I gave no reply
But slowly, sleepily:
'Wait a while yet! Wait a little!'
But 'yet' and 'yet' goes on and on,
And 'wait a little' grows too long.

(Medieval English Verse, trans. Brian Stone, Baltimore, Md., Penguin Books, 1964, p. 72)

10. Pray together

What spiritual issues of endings and waiting were raised as concerns in the session? Pray over them. Pray together for the power of your imaginations to help you cope, plan, and grow in the face of life's challenges.

CONNECTING WITH GOD

Read this poem about the experience of waiting. Who's waiting? How does it express "the other side" of apocalyptic anticipation?

NOTES

3

Tracking the Course of Change

Session Focus: Accelerating change characterizes our century and world. How do we cope and keep up? What are the values and the problems of living in a rapidly changing society? What do we need to hold on to for continuity in our lives? What do the social and technological changes of our time mean to the church?

Scriptures Used: Ecclesiastes 1; Revelation 21:5

BEFORE THE SESSION

Respond to these questions about your own experience of change.

1. I first became aware that time was quickly moving forward when I _____.

2. I am generally (circle one) enthusiastic/unenthusiastic about changes.

3. I have in_____ places so far in my life.

4. Probably the most important change in my life up to this point has been _____.

5. I feel that I (circle one) had a choice/had no choice in relationship to that change (4. above).

6. With the passing of time I feel (circle one) an increasing pressure/a diminishing pressure to change.

7. I am (circle one) pleased/not pleased with my relationship to change in my life.

Following God into the Future

Threat and Opportunity

As you read, meditate on these paragraphs about change.

We are finishing one century and beginning another in a time of accelerating social and technological change, both locally and globally. The social changes are so massive as to seemingly be a threat. Even when the changes seem good, they push us around and sometimes make us wonder how we will ever live with them. We are variously enchanted or chagrined by changes in sexuality: sexual revolution, feminism, gay and lesbian identity, and freedoms. We have been amazed at changes in nations: a united Germany, the breakup of the United Soviet Socialist Republic, new black leadership in South African government, nuclear power in India and Pakistan. Technological changes affect us daily. The "information highway" invites computers to manage and operate our communications, entertainment, transportation, and environmental systems (and more!). Changes in medicine, food production, and health care exude both social and technological ramifications. The changes come rapidly and often. One wonders sometimes how many of us long for the time when everything seemed simpler and our world seemed more stable.

How is it possible to keep up? If we buy all the upgrades for our computer software programs, we find ourselves having to buy new computer hardware as well. No sooner do we save enough money and buy something than we find there is a new, improved model (or version) in the marketplace and what we have just purchased needs updating or is already obsolete. We can almost handle the changes for ourselves, but sometimes we despair about how our (and society's) children and grandchildren will cope. How many of us ever wonder if we will even like these young people; they often seem so "different." (Just imagine how *we* seem to them!) We like watching movies on our VCR or DVD, but will we always have to ask friends to program the machine for us? Just what options do we need on our telephones? We have so many choices. Even someone changing lanes on the road too quickly in front of us can set us off and invite us to rage (to whatever degree) at the impoliteness or impudence.

Problems attend every new value our rapidly changing society presents. The new telephone conveniences increase the monthly bills. Cable television offers lots of programs and too many choices. We contrast the picture of an eager Abraham Lincoln poring over a few available books by firelight with our own blasé punching of the remote channel changer while we surf through fifty or more choices. The use of credit cards often leaves some people with a massive bill and the threat of bankruptcy. We pay a high price even to accommodate convenient and beneficial changes. Huge changes bring with them threats related to our well-being and our ability to keep up and thrive.

1. Check in on one another's changes

In small groups, talk briefly about some of your responses to the questionnaire above (see "Before the Session"). Give a general impression of your feelings about change. Let everyone contribute. Listen to one another carefully and ask questions for clarification.

2. Make true confessions

Which of the changes discussed in the article above ("Threat and Opportunity") do we have control over? How does the level of control affect our attitude toward the changes we experience? If we admit we have little or no control over such changes, how might this admission become part of our ability to cope?

3. Remember the past

Books and authors have always been concerned with the future. The best-selling book *Future Shock*

CONNECTING WITH ONE ANOTHER

Refer to the paragraphs above for this opening group discussion.

Choose one of these resources for discussion. If you are planning two sessions, use one book for each week.

predicted a future (our present) in which changes would be so massive, so rapid, so unanticipated, that the great challenge of living successfully and with good health would relate mostly to the ability to accommodate change. Many readers concede the author was right. Business, management, arts, philosophy, sociology, psychology, theology, and other disciplines embrace the theme of change at the center of their discussion. To get a sense of what changes are affecting you the most, think back to what you were doing in your work, or life, and in your family in 1970 when Alvin Toffler wrote *Future Shock*. What were your favorite activities? How do they compare to your current favorite things to do?

If Toffler's book nearly pre-dates you, try this one.

George Orwell projected an ominous future in his famous novel *1984*. Recall and tell what you were doing in your family, church, and community in 1984. Then, in one sentence, describe one major change in you that occurred in the recent or long-ago past.

4. Pray with one another

Make prayer requests relating to experiences of change that are most affecting your community. Offer these ideas as requests rather than items for discussion. Take time to gather them into a single request. For instance, a prayer leader could begin a prayer time with the words: "God, hear all the concerns we voice and the concerns behind them we are unable to speak." Allow for individual prayers to be spoken.

5. List synonyms for change

Brainstorm synonyms and phrases for change. When you have listed the expressions mentioned, ask the group to categorize them and establish "types" of change we encounter in life. Discuss how each category is different from the others. What one category might seem more challenging than the

CONNECTING WITH THE THEME

Provide a chart and marker for this activity.

others? Why? How does change affect you emotionally now compared to how it affected you earlier?

6. Cope with change

Ask one person to read aloud these paragraphs. Discuss the questions at the end as a group.

People make widely different responses to change, ranging from retreating from social interaction to embracing almost every change presenting itself. Due to their values, most people find themselves responding to change inconsistently, one time being in reaction and another time greeting change with open arms.

For a wide variety of reasons, numerous people give up on the public schools' ability to educate. The schools somehow do not reflect their values, either generally or specifically. As a result, some have adopted home schooling as the way to educate their young people. Others create private schools with a curriculum that more nearly meets their needs, as they perceive them. Some families, frustrated by social evils (or simply frustrated), quit watching television; others retreat from the city to the country. Even though these responses to perceived problems are in no way new, they announce that an individual or a group will make or adapt to changes in the way they judge best. All of this raises the issue of balancing between individual needs and needs for the good of the community.

What evaluations can be made for home schooling, private schooling, manipulation of media, or moves away from the mainstream? When do such responses seem good to you? When do you consider them detrimental? Why? What do we need to hold on to for continuity in our lives? In what ways have members of your group made varying adaptations to change?

7. Compare and contrast two biblical perspectives: Ecclesiastes 1:8–11; Revelation 21:5

Look at two very different biblical ideas.

The Bible has many viewpoints on the subject of change. Read these two Bible passages aloud as illustrations. Divide into two groups for the reading. Make the group selection process interesting. Work for balanced groups. Discuss the two passages for their similarities and differences. What do you imagine accounts for the difference? What kind of group or personal situation may be reflected in each reading? How do the readings relate to your own past week? How do they relate to your group, to your congregation, or to your larger community? What significance do you find in the appearance of such diverse responses to change in the Bible?

8. Apply change theory to your life 🗝

CONNECTING WITH LIFE

"Change" is now a major topic in library filing systems. One can find books in sociology, philosophy, art, education, business, psychology, and history in the "change" listing. Business may have the most intense interest in change, perhaps due to the cutting–edge challenges to tradition that characterize the business world. What drives change (both individual and corporate)? When do we push it or stop it? Why? When do we have or take control? The consciousness of change in business has led to hundreds of books and seminars to help entrepreneurs and managers maximize professional effectiveness in work and avocations in order to increase profitability and enhance success.

Business-related books may be of interest to non-business people because of their pragmatic point of view, often dealing directly with the theory and consequences of change. The practical applications may encourage us to initiate changes in our personal lives as well as in our affiliations. Many writers agree with author Liz Clarke when she asserts, "There is, in fact, no significant difference between organizational change and personal change." (Liz Clarke, *The Essence of Change,* Prentice Hall, Englewood Cliffs, N.J., 1994, p. 73.) With this in mind, let us examine an important change concept gleaned from business theory.

Rupert Eales-White writes, "In a world of change, asking the right question is more important than finding the 'right' answer. 'Right' answers can be wrong, because they may answer the wrong question." (*Creating Growth from Change*, McGraw-Hill Book Company, Berkshire, England, 1994, p. 4.)

If we are to ask the right question, we need to think about options that are open to us in the light of change. We then move beyond liking or disliking the perceived changes to imagining alternative responses and outcomes. We ask about our needs as individuals and groups:

- ▲ Why do we need to be able to predict the future?

- ▲ In what ways can we accommodate ourselves to uncertainty?

- ▲ When do we need to set a goal?

- ▲ Why may it serve us to envision several outcomes?

By approaching the changes and their effects on us, we can ask questions about the situations and about ourselves that potentially lead us to unanticipated resolutions or accommodations.

9. Chart your change areas

"'Change' means changing our attitude to risk. We must be prepared to take risks that we would not normally contemplate." (Rupert Eales-White, p. 4) Divide a paper into four sections by drawing lines or folding. Mark one section "family," one "work," one "church," one "life goal." Think about the risk factors in each of these change areas in your life. Draw a picture, diagram, symbol, or write a word that summarizes or captures an intention, feeling, challenge, or goal in each of the sections. Visualize one of the

Following God into the Future

risks implied in an attempt to make the changes you desire. As you feel open, show the diagram to another individual in the group. Explain the idea, and ask the other person to support you in thought and prayer in the weeks to come.

10. Apply change theory to the life of the church

Meditate on this quote and consider its potential.

"When we think of the world's future, we always mean the destination it will reach if it keeps going in the direction we can see it going in now; it does not occur to us that its path is not a straight line but a curve, constantly changing direction." (Ludwig Witgenstein, *Culture and Value,* ed. G. H. von Wright, The University of Chicago Press, Chicago, Ill., 1980, p. 3). The same may be said of the church. Think about the following assertions and questions and then break into groups to follow the process outlined below.

▲ Figuring out what to do with change means making accurate projections for our congregation's future. How will we be able to find projections we can agree on and commit ourselves to?

▲ Figuring out what to do with change means wondering what risks are most worthwhile for us to take. What standards do we use to evaluate what risks are worth taking?

▲ Figuring out what to do with change means asking the right questions of the future. Who is asking unusual and creative questions in our group or church right now?

In small groups discuss change factors and risks that face your church. Recall your findings and suggestions with the total group.

In groups of four (or all together, if your group is small) discuss and write down some questions that need to be asked about changes taking place in your congregation. Identify some changes. Choose one to focus on. Begin by discussing the questions currently being asked in relation to the situation. Then pose new questions that could refocus the discussion. List the risks that such questions pose for the church. In each group, or as a total group, agree on one or two of the questions and risks and strategize new ways to bring them to the attention of the congregation (e.g., presentations, proposals, board meetings, sermons, lessons, articles).

11. Read a litany of change

Leader: God, we are overwhelmed with change.

Readers: Help us remember your plan to make all things new in your time.

Leader: We try to cope with social changes and feel inadequate, resistant, resentful, or sometimes hopeful.

Readers: Anchor us somehow through it all:

Leader: emerging nationalities,

Readers: re-united Germany,

Leader: un-united Czech and Slovak Republics,

Readers: black leadership in South African government;

Leader: new racial understandings;

Readers: the unrelenting population explosion;

Leader: technological changes,

Readers: our move into the information generation,

Leader: computers changing almost everything;

Readers: new procedures in medicine, surgery, intervention;

Leader: changes in food production,

Readers: in mechanical production,

Leader: in labor,

Readers: in communications.

Leader: Our list goes on;

Readers: our prayer never ends.

Leader: May our lives be enriched by the new;

Readers: May we be sustained in your love and creativity.

Leader: Hear our prayer. Amen.
Readers: We pray in Jesus' name. Amen.

12. Pray for the church

Using prayer requests from earlier in the session and responding to the discussions above, close your session by offering prayers for the future of the church and its members in the face of change.

4

From Generation to Generation

Session Focus: How do we hand down the faith and a decent life to those who are younger than we or not yet born? Decisions we make and opportunities we provide affect the possible outcome for our children in the faith. Our stewardship of time and resources influences not only this time, but future generations as well.

Scriptures Used: Deuteronomy 6:4–6, 20–25; Psalm 78:1–8

Read and consider your relationship with these experiences and ideas.

People usually have goals to leave something to someone else (e.g., to friends, family, children, institutions). If people have enough resources, they often save some of them to benefit others. They invest various resources of time and money in many things (e.g., education). A fortunate few set up trust funds for their offspring, other relatives, and the like or otherwise amass an estate as an inheritance. Most parents, and adults in general, try to make life better for their children and others they care about. So it is in the life of faith. People of faith want others to have faith. But just what kind of faith? What do they mean by faith, and how can they accomplish this goal?

Educator John H. Westerhoff III's writings provide a nice focus for our consideration of the matter of passing on (handing down) faith. His contrast of faith and religion is helpful in that it clarifies just what an older generation can pass on to the younger, and how. He asserts,

> Faith cannot be taught by any method of instruction....We can only teach religion. We can know about religion, but we can only expand in faith, act in faith, and live in faith. Faith can be inspired within a community of faith, but it cannot be given to one person by another. Faith is expressed, transformed, and made meaningful by persons sharing their faith in an historical, tradition-bearing community of faith." (John H. Westerhoff III, *Will Our Children Have Faith?* The Seabury Press, New York, N.Y., 1976, p. 23.)

Micah 6:6–8

Biblical tradition develops ideas of the kind of faith we can pass on to other generations. The prophets of Israel criticized people's acceptance of "right ritual" as faith. Micah insisted that faithful children of God would do more than make the right sacrifices at the right time (this latter is what Westerhoff would call religion). They also would be just and merciful. We can perhaps critique Christian people's acceptance of "right understanding" as the essence of faith. We realize that the faith we want to pass on will go beyond being able to parrot the right answers to standard questions. We wish that faith (of those we pass it on to) to be actual experiences, concepts, and feelings that transform their living. We, too, will insist on qualities like mercy, humility, and justice.

We must go beyond notions of simply handing down something, as if we were giving another person a gift on a birthday or leaving an inheritance. We are not handing down anything in a literal sense, but rather we are hoping to live in such faithful ways as to intrigue others with our lives. We want them to value and, as appropriate, to support and continue the organizations we create(d). We wish them to be faithful to the God and Christ whose names we invoke. We are interested in their observing the values we live by, so that they, too, will experiment with them and give themselves wholeheartedly to the God of justice and love.

1. Praise your heroes

Think back for a few moments on what adults played an important role in your childhood and youth faith development. What experiences stand out as most important? Who were the actors? Who contributed the most to you, and how so? What ideas can you glean from these experiences as you consider your position as an adult with responsibility toward the young?

In the group, describe one such experience each. Discuss the ideas that occurred to you as you reflected on your experience and that occur to you as you hear others' experiences.

2. Pray as a group

Include in your prayer time today your concerns for the growth of young people in your church and community. Intercede on behalf of the schools, the church schools, youth groups, and other community-based youth organizations. Pray for leaders and young people by name.

3. Discuss our responsibility

Responsibilities of parenting, grandparenting, mentoring, and caregiving seem apparent, at least when viewed generally. Of course, any parent, grandparent, mentor, or caregiver in action is faced with the realization that the details of how to carry out this responsibility are often quite unclear. For those adults in a community who do not have children in

CONNECTING WITH ONE ANOTHER

Reflect in silence. Discuss your own faith development. If the group is large, subdivide for the discussion.

CONNECTING WITH THE THEME

As a group, clarify the responsibility older persons carry for younger.

Following God into the Future

their direct care, the responsibility is more generalized and even more difficult to act upon with certainty. Teachers may have a clear understanding of their task but sometimes find themselves in conflict with the primary caregivers. Distant relatives, friends of a family, sponsors, neighbors all have some responsibility. It takes a village to raise a child. In fact, all adults have at least a generalized responsibility. Laws must be fair toward the young. Use of resources must keep their future in sight. The older are responsible toward the younger, the stronger for the weaker. Remember the faith village!

Discuss these questions.

▲ What are we doing right now to help equip our children, grandchildren, students, and youngsters?

▲ How can we help young people make good decisions?

▲ How can we tell the difference between when we are helping and when we are hurting others?

▲ How do our attitudes toward the future help or hinder those we parent or mentor or care for?

▲ What clues do our young people give us regarding our success at passing on the faith and a decent life?

4. Pass on my faith? ◁▭

Discuss these questions and paragraphs in your group. Subdivide if your group is large so everyone has a chance to talk as well as listen.

What makes us think we have a faith worth handing down or a decent life ourselves? How do we understand faith and character? What mistakes would we hope others could avoid making? These important questions confront us as we consider what we may hope to instill in others. Faith has to do with the ability to live a life of some quality, interpreted in the light of symbols of the Divine. We give life religious value and find it helpful to do so. On this basis we assume such a life will be of value, especially to the next generation. But how do we know if that is so?

Recall the different kinds of faith between our parents' experience and our own. Remembering and clarifying such differences can help us focus on the process of faithful living that brings hope, meaning, and power into one's experience. If our faith is different from our parents' faith, we anticipate the faith we pass on may eventually be different from our own.

Since faith can be understood in a larger context than we ordinarily tend to consider, we may want to broaden the discussion far beyond what our church or even our families do together. The whole of life is the arena in which faith is played out. Rapid change affects the way in which we project the faith experience of another generation. In what area of your life have you found your faith surprisingly helpful or meaningful? Why are you surprised? What did you expect differently?

The concept of a decent life bears examination. Decency usually suggests conformity to standards of taste, propriety, or quality. In a faith context, we must opt for standards of quality over standards of taste or propriety. Tastes change. Proprieties of one generation may ring false to another generation. Exactly what do we mean by the quality of life we want other generations to enjoy? Advantages such as education, success, freedom, health, opportunity, and choice may express the notion of quality. What might you add to the list?

5. Discuss education for the future

The general discussion of preparing students for the future can clarify our concerns for faith education and the hope for a decent life.

Read this summary of one person's thought about preparing youth for the future.

There is...in our schools, a tendency to carry from the past what was learned in the past, to bring along what served past generations. Much of this is undoubtedly of value, particularly in conveying to students the vital awareness that they are part of an extended historical human

Following God into the Future

family to whom they are indebted for much of what they are and have today. Yet the heritage of the past is not sufficient preparation for the years of life which lie in the future, and as that future brings wider and faster change it is less and less adequate. (Leon Martel, *Mastering Change*, Simon & Schuster, Inc., New York, N.Y., 1986, p. 165.)

One of Martel's concerns (he is a business teacher) centers on how education in the schools is a reflection of needs for industrialization. In our post-industrial age, schools and education must proceed in new ways. As one might expect, Martel emphasizes the need in school curriculum for science, math, communications, robotics, alternative energy sources, environmental protection, and bioscience.

But by far the largest need—in terms of numbers to be served—will be for the education of all the nonspecialists who in their own careers, and in their daily lives as well, will need knowledge of the concepts, capabilities, and operations of the new products of science and technology. (Martel, p. 66)

Other topics of extreme importance to Martel are related to broadening our understanding of other cultures for the purpose of learning from the whole world of human experience. Finally, he concludes,

Our greatest need in dealing with change will be the need to innovate, to creatively make us into what is new and different. In the humanities, above all, is found the creativity of mankind [sic]—sometimes in a carefully ordered way, as in a [poetic] sonnet or a [musical] fugue, at other times in an almost uncontrolled surge of emotion, like an expressionist painting or a frenzied religious dance; but always with a message, or in a form, that arrests our attention and places in our minds something that was not there before. It is this quality of creativity that we will especially need in order to master future change. (Martel, p. 68)

Consider how Martel's ideas can help us provide effective Christian education with a bias toward the future.

The tendency to conceive of education as bringing to the present the ideas and skills of the past is also true in our church schools and other religious education institutions. Martel's discussion takes on even more weight when we recall that the church school movement started in newly industrialized England just over 200 years ago. The church has rarely thought of educating its young to deal with a changing world. Today we need to be alert to the church school's weaknesses as well as its strengths as an educational approach and institution. How can we change it to adequately project a vital faith vision that will carry our youngsters through the challenges of their changing lives in a changing world?

Discuss how Martel's ideas can help us make plans and changes in the church.

Which of Martel's ideas about education in the arts and humanities relates to what the church can provide for its members? What would the consideration of faith education as equipping our young people to cope effectively with the future do for the way we organize and plan? What kinds of approaches would get your priority? What kinds of activities do you imagine would be the most helpful? Can these activities be accomplished in a one-hour Sunday morning classroom setting? What parts of the Bible would be most significant in such a venture?

6. Look for ideas

Deuteronomy 6:4–7, 20–25.

Highlight or note on a piece of paper words or phrases of this Bible passage that reflect your values or give you an idea about the effective, change-oriented faith education of young people. An option might be writing group responses, as the text is read, on newsprint or a large sheet of paper and posting it on a wall or back of a door for review and reflection by the group.

Discuss both the ideas noted during the reading and the following ideas. What history can you imagine would be meaningful for young people today? What stories from the Bible, from national life, from world history, and from current events seem most important? Which ones promise to be most potent to interpret your values and religious commitments? How do these stories relate to ceremonial and ritual life in the church, home, and community? Which ones are actually part of your church's teaching of the young?

Compare and discuss your markings.

7. List potentials 🔑

How do we actually pass along our faith? When do we teach? Besides providing educational classes in the church, how else do we teach, value, and pass along our best? Write down an idea or instance for each category listed below. Indicate an experience or a reflection to gain insight into the process.

CONNECTING WITH LIFE

Jot down ideas.

When finished, relate your responses.

▲ educational classes or groups

▲ toy purchases

▲ television channels

▲ religious participation

▲ daily schedules

▲ activities

▲ personal budget

▲ volunteer time

8. Consider your church's values

Have copies of your church's budget or be sure to have church allocations for Christian education, membership, and other program areas.

How does your church's budget (the procedures, the capital projects, the line items) and cooperation with regional or area entities to provide special programming interpret current commitments regarding faith nurturing? What strategies might help the congregation take certain needs even more seriously? How does your faith community plan to pass on the faith? The stewardship of time and resources influences not only the present but future generations as well.

9. Clarify your thinking 🔑

Play with objections to hand-me-downs.

Reconsider your interest in helping future generations. These days there is an issue of style with hand-me-downs. Some of us are so style conscious that we will not wear last year's fashions, whether they were handed down or purchased new. The whole notion of hand-me-downs highlights values in experience. The expression of handing down something may have distasteful inferences—of larger to smaller, of mature to immature, of tried to untried, of superior to inferior. In clothing, our most common use of the idea, hand-me-downs occur when a sibling or friend has outgrown a piece of clothing. This garment is then given to a younger person to wear until it is no longer wearable or is outgrown and handed down to another wearer. How does this help focus your concerns for a vital faith in the next generation (a faith to pass on)? How do your objections to some of the possible implications clarify your goals and decisions on behalf of others?

10. Pray a scripture 🔑

CONNECTING WITH GOD

Be sure everyone has a pencil or pen to mark a favorite phrase or line during the reading.

Divide the group in half to read aloud Psalm 78:1–8. One half reads the first phrase of each verse, the other half the second phrase. When finished reading, invite participants to say aloud the words or phrases they found most meaningful and why. Incorporate these into a prayer for the faith of future generations.

11. Close with prayer

Request participants to offer their concerns for the future of the faith of others or pray together, using the ideas from the opening of the session.

NOTES

5

Living in Exile

Session Focus: Because of rapid changes, increased mobility, family redefinition, and so much more, people today often feel they are in exile from their own past. How can one live creatively in this "exile" and reclaim and redefine one's faith for the present time?

Scriptures Used: Ezekiel 10, 12, 37

BEFORE THE SESSION

As you read, recall how this story may be like and unlike your own.

The little man with beautiful brown skin came to worship. He insisted he was in the right place, although the sponsors who helped bring him to America had assumed he would go to another church. "This church," Narin insisted. He came to our church because he could read the word Christian in the name on the sign out front. He was one of dozens of Cambodians who were resettled in our town and one of thousands resettled in America in the late 1980s.

One of the church greeters came to get me, supposing somehow that I would be able to understand him. I tried but could not. Over the next months Narin attended our church. Through our time together in worship and my visits to his home, we became friends. Even though his French-laced English improved, we could never quite trust our understanding of one another. Eventually, I grasped some of the story of this man living in a strange new land.

The Cambodian government had been taken over by the Khmer Rouge under the leadership of Pol Pot, and Narin's family's life was changed. Overnight his wife became a rice farmer. Until then she had been waited on by servants. For years the couple had enjoyed weekend trips to luxury hotels, fancy meals, and ballroom dancing in Thailand. Now his wife was farming in a rural commune, and no one knew where Narin was. Fortunately, Narin's father had helped many people over the years through his medical practice. These people helped Narin escape three times although he had been arrested and was to be killed. He escaped to the relative safety of a refugee camp on the Thai border. Eventually his wife and son joined him there.

They lost everything they owned: houses and automobiles, gold and diamonds, family and prestige. In the camp they set out to make a new life. In America they continued this journey. Their story of change and adaptation gave me insight into my own life and my own experience of change. Today, many years later, I still understand these things as imperfectly as I then grasped Narin's English. Narin and his family did come to a right place both for themselves and for me. His life and witness changed my perspective and enriched my experience.

A time of rapid change

The lives of countless people in all parts of the world change dramatically with wars, migrations, and other disasters. Because of the present rapidity (and the sheer number) of changes, many people who never have experienced a war, a coup, an earthquake, a tornado, or a similar calamity still feel as if their world is now devastated. Perhaps their search for a new job has moved them away from familiar territory. Their constant mobility has made it impossible to even feel that they have a family or can dare put down roots. Due to divorces, family changes, altering values, developing tastes, and new social movements, people today often feel that they are in exile from their own pasts.

1. Inventory your changes 🔑

Make a list of major changes for you in your lifetime: changes that affected the way you do things, or caused you to relocate, or that made you into a different person. Add to the list changes that created new possibilities in your work, your education, and your knowledge.

Decide in small groups which one of these changes was the most influential in the lives of most of the people in each group. State your conclusion(s) to the total group. Discuss your ideas together.

2. Pray for the world

In prayer, focus on unsettling events in the news (e.g., a recent atrocity committed in the name of nationalism, the inhumanity of one group against another, the pain of a natural disaster, a news event evoking sadness and begging for intercession). Tell one another how these events affect you. Describe your feelings, your hopes, how the events relate emotionally to your own experiences of loss. Pray for strength, vision, commitment, and wisdom.

3. Consider an ancient exile 🔑

The Jewish exile in Babylon resulted from a terrible tragedy, but it called the Jews to one of the most creative periods of their history. Theirs was a tiny country sitting in the main traffic corridor between Babylon and Egypt. Eventually the alliances that protected them failed. The Jews found the Babylonian army at their gates and watched in grief

CONNECTING WITH ONE ANOTHER

Divide into sub-groups and list changes of a lifetime.

Search current newspapers for information or reminders.

CONNECTING WITH THE THEME

Read this summary of the destruction and rebirth of ancient Judah.

Following God into the Future

and agony as their villages, their cities, and even their beautiful temple burned. Jewish leaders were carried off to other countries, and outsiders came to run their government. Their own prophets had warned of these possibilities. Some understood the devastation to be a judgment from God. Their unfaithfulness was surely the cause of the catastrophe. A few Jewish prophets and leaders also talked about a restoration. They were sure God meant to create a new nation in which ancient promises of prosperity and faithfulness would be realized. Under the encouragement of these newer prophets, the Jews found redemption through a new identity.

Surely they were surprised that this new identity was unrelated to their promised land. They redefined a new oneness and faith in the experience of exile. No longer could they turn toward the temple in Jerusalem. If they did, it only brought tears and sadness. They learned to sing God's songs in a new land with a new self-understanding that incorporated a creative retelling of their story and its promise. God was doing a new thing in history and in their community. The Jews who eventually moved back to Jerusalem and the old Judah came back with a fresh understanding of what it meant to be the people of the living God.

Discuss these questions.

How can we today live creatively "in exile" and reclaim and redefine our faith for the present time? How do different cultural groups continue to experience a sense of being "in exile"? How do modern stories of various minority and ethnic groups compare with that of Judah?

4. Read about life-giving change

Think on this contrast of ancient and current experiences.

Life takes on new meaning after any apocalypse. What today is called Judaism has its roots in the Babylonian exile. After their return to Jerusalem, Jews never again lived in the same way as before.

Though they rebuilt the temple, they wept at how insignificant it seemed in comparison to Solomon's great temple of the past. Along with the new temple sprang up synagogues, like the ones that served the people in exile. These new places of study and prayer transformed the understanding of temple worship itself and its place in Jewish life. The reading of the Law was done in the old way, but the interpretation changed. Yes, the people were happy to be back home again, but that old home was not the same one their parents and grandparents left years earlier. The returning people brought changed attitudes, expectations, habits, and perceptions. Ancient Judah was living beyond the end of Jerusalem and into a new experience of being the people of God.

The church similarly lived beyond the experience of the second end of Jerusalem in 70 C.E. Herein may rest the origin of the church's consciousness of itself as the "new Israel," the new temple, a newly described people of God. The church viewed itself as a "remnant" of its Jewish background.

We now live beyond the end of what some name "Christian Europe." Many churches on other continents send missionaries to work in European cities. The church in North America also lives beyond the experience of being a Christian majority. Countries are sending missionaries to North America now. Yes, Christian and Jewish ideals may prevail in law and in common life, but there are other voices speaking with increasing volume and influence. These new voices are metamorphosing the way Christians see and experience themselves and the world.

A new status for the Jews affected their development. They worked in the new environment, finding favor, surviving attack, gaining insights into God's life and their own possibilities. We, too, can change and grow.

The Jews redefined their worship in the experience of exile. How has modern experience rede-

Respond to these questions for discussion.

Following God into the Future

fined worship in your church? What important new-ness pervades the worship experiences in churches in your city or area?

The Jewish exile redefined Jewish heritage. Jews still understood themselves as children of Abraham, but they also had a new experience. In what ways may modern Christians seem exiled? How has life at the end of the twentieth century brought on a feeling of exile for many people? What symbols of religious conviction have you had to give up? What hopes have you relinquished and what new hopes now sustain you? How have the losses and gains made you stronger to meet the challenges of the present? What does it mean to you to say you are a child of God?

5. Tell your story

In small groups, briefly tell stories of "exile." Relate aspects of the past you are happy to be rid of, lost things that you mourn, things you feel you would like to regain, or values you want to pass on to others. Delight in the telling and the hearing. Perhaps even create a real or imaginative setting for your group to tell the stories (e.g., a dusk campfire scene, a family or school reunion, a retirement party, an anniversary celebration).

6. Consider an ancient oracle 🔑

Project Ezekiel's place into our own time.

Ezekiel represents the prophetic movement in the two centuries preceding the founding of Christianity. He was critical of the societal status quo. His vantage point was almost ethereal. Ezekiel described getting there as being lifted up by his hair and placed on a high mountain. From there he could look over the historical landscape of past, present, and the immediate future. Philosopher Kenneth Burke writes about this envisioning process.

The desire to re-characterize events necessarily requires a new reading of the signs—and though men have ever 'looked backwards,' the backward looking of the 'prophets' is coupled with a new principle of interpretation, a new perspective or point of view, whereby the picture of 'things as they really are' is reorganized. (*Permanence and Change,* University of California Press, Berkeley and Los Angeles, Calif., 1965, p. 180.)

Ask three groups to each read one of the Ezekiel chapters and give the entire group highlights of the prophetic vision.

Ezekiel 10, Ezekiel 12, Ezekiel 37

Three of Ezekiel's visions may provide a basis for understanding how a group of people may live beyond destruction. In Ezekiel 10 the oracle recounts the vision of when God's glory left Jerusalem. Ezekiel 12 records that the destruction was no longer to be postponed. God had grown too tired of the unfaithful attitudes and actions of people who should have known better. Perhaps most familiar of all the visions (the story of the dry bones), Ezekiel 37 tells that new life is a possibility for Israel; the divided nations will have a new, united identity. "Ezekiel is the prophet of imagination....He imagined both exile and redemption in ways that made them both tangible." (Elie Wiesel, in *Congregation: Contemporary Writers Read the Jewish Bible*, ed. by David Rosenberg, Harcourt Brace Jovanovich, San Diego, Calif., 1987, p. 169.)

Several modern situations present catastrophes that result in displacement, new self-understandings, and massive changes. Jews who witnessed and survived the Nazi holocaust now write of a new identity and of the necessity for world change. Other challenges include the Khmer Rouge regime suffered by Cambodians, the worldwide devastation caused by AIDS, the civil war destruction in Eastern Europe, and the ongoing tensions in Asia. How can groups live beyond massive destruction? What hope does Ezekiel's example hold out? What kind of backward and forward looks can we fashion? What new readings of these historical signs can we make? How can we speak words of encouragement?

Make applications
to your work and
life experiences.

Discuss these
questions.

Silently
contemplate your
life and list how you
are living after
change.

7. Talk about work and life

Discuss changes within your workplace (or the workplaces of others you know) and life that have left you with feelings of being out of touch, out of sync with the company, institution, or environment. Maybe these are small changes, such as those discussed by Rupert Eales-White: "criticism or praise, requests from our boss, being presented with a *fait accompli*, being late for an important meeting, being flattered and imposed upon, a proposal or idea from a subordinate, interruptions, a rude client." (Eales-White, pp. xi, xii.)

How do such changes and the feelings accompanying them affect your ability to function with the group or within the context of your vocation or avocation or life? What creative changes have resulted from the group's accommodation to larger changes such as cost cutting, a new mission or purpose, new goals, or new structures and systems? How different is your self-understanding as a result of the accommodation?

8. Life after change

One recently divorced man talked of his experience. No longer was he part of a couple. With the retraction of a vow, he was a single person. In a conference he said, "I can no longer assume that I am supplemented by my spouse. I can no longer invite someone into my life knowing they will benefit from my wife's life. I am on my own." From this awareness he was able to begin rebuilding his life.

On a piece of paper, list the things in flux in your life. Begin with conventional issues and experiences (e.g., profession, avocation, marriage, location, acquaintances, religious practices). Consider how your identity is in flux alongside these. For example, what personal perceptions are in flux in your religious life? Finally, what is changing in what you may call your "social location"? Some people may be identifying with a new group (e.g., a church, a minority). What instituted these changes? How are they in the process of changing? How do you align with these situations (e.g., life after children leave home, life with a new job or vocation, life with no job, life with loss of spouse, life with death of loved ones, life with one's own chronic illness). Keep this list private. Between now and the next group gathering, think about what you are experiencing and what you want.

9. Describe a resurrection

Wiesel indicates that all the visions in Ezekiel are dated, except the one of the valley of the dry bones.

> ...meaning that the resurrection is undated. And we understand why: that vision, that promise, that hope, is not linked to either space or time. That vision, that consolation, is offered to every generation, for every generation needs it—and ours more than any before us. (Elie Wiesel, p. 186)

Discuss this quote in relation to happenings in your group over the past few weeks.

10. Meditate on your need for resurrection

▲ As with many other people in the world, I, too, have met with displacement, disappointment, and the accompanying despair. (*pause*)

▲ In the light of Jewish survival in ancient and modern times, I, too, affirm the possibility of meaningful and hopeful life beyond an apocalypse. (*pause*)

▲ I think about ways I can affirm my belief in resurrection and enter into a new life. (*pause*)

Spend a few minutes in contemplation while one person reads and pauses between the following sentences.

11. Pray together

Close the session with prayers that include the concerns voiced in the session. Give everyone an

Following God into the Future

opportunity to pray aloud and then close the session with the repetition of the Lord's Prayer in unison. You may wish to use this modernized version.

Our Father in heaven,
hallowed be your Name,
your kingdom come,
your will be done,
on earth as in heaven.

Give us today our daily bread.
Forgive us our sins
as we forgive those
who sin against us.

Save us from the time of trial,
and deliver us from evil.

For the kingdom, the power,
and the glory are yours,
now and for ever. Amen.

(Chalice Hymnal, Chalice Press, St. Louis, Mo., 1995, p. 775. Used by permission.)

6

Following God into the Future

Session Focus: The question "What will the future bring?" invites amazing conjecture. This session focuses on images of the future that we expect to arise from our faith. From faith experiences and images we will seek to answer how we can build our own and our church's best future.

Scriptures Used: Isaiah 60:1–5; 64:1–8

BEFORE THE SESSION

Read and reflect.

What will the future bring? For some people this question is full of disconcerting things. For the confident, the answer includes some form of hopefulness. For many in the Euro-American world, it may pick up the baggage of nearly two hundred and fifty years of wondering what the year 2000 will bring. It calls up images of space travel, strange extraterrestrial creatures, mysticism, humor, and horror. It often presents high-tech advantages paired with low-tech dread.

Jules Verne (1828–1905), creator of the science fiction novel genre, successfully melded adventure and rational scientific description. So many writers follow his lead that now one can shop bookstores entirely dedicated to science fiction.

Put schematically, science fiction writing began from a technological and ethnocentric base in

1850, and by the start of the 1960s it had succeeded in exploring and categorizing the future in ways that were both convincing and comprehensive. Throughout this period, writers ventured into a more or less pagan future for humanity, and brought back kaleidoscopic and bustling visions...lightning flashes of truth in the social, sexual, psychic and technological domains, within space and within the infinity of time. (Christophe Canto and Odile Faliu, *The History of the Future: Images of the 21st Century*, trans. Francis Cowper, Flammarion, 1993, p. 14.)

Science fiction sets the tone for most current imaginations of the future.

Even if one never reads science fiction, one has probably seen a sci-fi movie. Often the imagery of these movies is medieval European, without explicit Christian trappings. Are we to read the imagery as metaphorical, or are we to believe the stories reject Christian values? Why is it difficult for science fiction to use common Christian symbols? What happens to Christian possibility in a future as portrayed in these stories? Why do writers not champion a Christian future?

If not all, certainly most sci-fi imaginations of humankind and the world see space as an important arena for the future. *Star Trek, Star Wars 2001: A Space Odyssey*, and other movies deal with a variety of species—human, subhuman, and superhuman. Robots are a constant companion in this new world of computers, space travel, time warp, and wild imaginings. Among the realities threatened in these futures are the end of humankind, the demise of the earth, the takeover by technology, or the beginning of a new age. Some hopeful images (e.g., *Star Trek*) contrast with many apocalyptic stories (e.g., *Mad Max*).

What images of the future can we expect from our faith? How can we build our personal and our church's best future? How do technological and bio-medical issues affect our faith (the prolongation of life, dealing with chronic illnesses, genetic manipulation, cloning, and the like)?

1. A survey

Circle the appropriate response.

Y   N   I think our group will greet the new millennium.

Y   N   We may still be using resources from this series.

Y   N   My family will be dispersed.

Y   N   Our church will be growing at its present rate.

Mark the following issues of the course that will have a direct impact on the group's makeup and common life: (briefly explain "how")

____ space travel

____ computer technology

____ robots

____ education of children

____ increased mobility of population

____ communication with extraterrestrial life

2. Tell favorite science fiction movie scenes

Spend a few minutes as a group telling your favorite scene. Even if you dislike science fiction, you still may recall a favorite scene in one or two movies. Try to offer one sentence that explains what makes the scene your favorite. Was it an unusual image, a great line, the reminder of a life event, humor,

By yourself, fill in this survey about your group. Spend a few minutes comparing answers.

Enjoy a brief conversation time.

Following God into the Future

silliness, or a deep meaning? Give each person a chance to briefly respond.

3. Pray together in the group

Share future-oriented concerns.

Today highlight issues and experiences that seem future oriented, especially in the biomedical or communications areas. For example, you may hold in your concerns (1) a person with a heart or kidney transplant, (2) cloning issues, (3) DNA manipulation enterprises, (4) in-vitro pregnancies. Pray for medical, technological, and public leaders to dialogue with one another, for justice to be wise, for wisdom in dealing with life-prolonging options. Pray for the equitable use of public resources in communications and health care.

4. Analyze a movie 🗝

CONNECTING WITH THE THEME

Use these ideas and others in "Enriching the Experience: Go to the Movies" (p. 76) to talk about a movie or movie scene.

Discuss a science fiction movie of the group's choosing from the points of view of the preceding chapters. Find out which movie most of the group has seen. If there is too little common experience, ask a few people who have seen the same movie to begin the discussion in a kind of "group fishbowl." As they discuss the issues, others who have not seen the movie can ask for clarification and detail. Starters could be how the movie...

- ▲ deals with images of the end
- ▲ presents a spiritual perspective of conflict
- ▲ portrays the theme of living in or after exile
- ▲ interprets education for change
- ▲ profiles theories of change
- ▲ uses important symbols
- ▲ alludes to other movies

In the discussion, try to intersect with current concerns.

If one were planning to enter the future the

movie depicts, what skills, survival tactics, interpersonal strengths, and so on would one start to develop in preparation? How do these ideas serve as a metaphor for present decision making? What kinds of community did the movie portray? How can its vision serve as a metaphor for the church in the world today? What are the movie's issues of integration, separation, or experimental community?

5. Update scriptural images

The last chapters of Isaiah search for hope within apocalyptic assumptions. Returnees from Babylon were living a desperate life. They saw its challenges related to a larger context of heavenly conflict. Isaiah's poem sometimes expects cataclysmic destruction.

Paraphrase some of the lines from Isaiah 60 so they pick up a current or future flavor or meaning. For instance, "for darkness shall cover the earth" could be paraphrased "for nuclear winter will freeze the earth's surface." Use your imagination.

Work in pairs to paraphrase parts of Isaiah 60:1–5. Read and discuss your suggestions in the group.

When finished sharing your paraphrases, ask what you discovered about the poem that helps you move toward a hopeful future. Compare these Isaiah verses to the opening words of Genesis 1. Play with the images of light and darkness to discover potentials of God's creative energy in your own experience and that of the church. How does this creative power reassert itself in community life?

6. Affirm the future

As creative persons, we live in a meaningful world of images (i.e., relationships, words, arts, fleeting imaginations, thoughts, feelings). These images help us to make decisions when challenged, hold on when feeling vulnerable, and move into an uncertain future. Affirmations are an important form these images can take. Listed below are several affirmations for the future.

CONNECTING WITH LIFE

Make affirmations about the future.

Following God into the Future

▲ As mom and dad used to say, "Things will be better in the morning."

▲ God is leading me into a future in which I will be able to realize my full potential.

▲ Although I will encounter many challenges, in the end I will find God sufficient for my needs.

▲ As I bring my life into line with the Divine will, I will manifest goodness in my life and in the lives of those around me.

▲ God's people are sustained and led into a glorious future by the Divine Presence.

▲ Since life presents possibilities for good and evil, I influence my own future by the choices I make.

▲ Ultimately, God will redeem and transform everything.

Take time to make your affirmations. Mark the affirmation you find most meaningful or challenging. Read your favorite to the group. Keep tabs on the most important or most often chosen affirmations. Talk together about what your affirmation means to you (and to the group), how it helps you, what changes it suggests, how it brings you hope.

7. Affirming your own changes

Because it is often difficult for us as adults in church to permit information or processes to actually change us, we may need to make affirmations of change that are distinctly theological. We can benefit from constructing what some call a "piety of change." In another time, one's piety was defined by church attendance, participation in prayer, service to neighbor, and other such things. The exact content of how one recognizes devotion in oneself or another changes over the years, but the need to understand is still there. What would a piety focused on change entail in our day? With images of a changing God, piety might focus on human change, the encounter with God in the process of change, the holiness of difference, and the move toward multiplicity. Conversion in such a context would be seen as dynamic, less controlled by the end product.

A church group may take on the cellular aspects of change—reproduction (division, growth, and so on). What could be missing in such cell groups is the need to nurture intimacy. The idea that a group will build trust and then split seems contrary to the common assumptions of the nature of human need and group health.

Traditionally, piety has been expressed in images of permanence, and these images are expressed as end result, perfection, goal, and so on. We call ourselves to examine the ways in which God is encountered on the road. How do we have intimacy? We establish God first and then open ourselves to receive and give gifts of intimacy. But this is all "strong" talk. I think I am strong. I believe many disciples also are strong. The intimacy is with God, with lovers, with family, with friends. We are strongly individualistic.

Piety comprises a sense and actuality of holiness, godliness, and devoutness.

8. Analyze and express your changes

Yes, we are on a path. Each of us has a story of this path. Tell it. Share your vision of life in change to challenge, suggest, strengthen, encourage, and invite others in your group to join you on the journey. What is your individual process of change, your individual commitment to change?

In groups of two or three, relate some happenings right now in your life.

- ▲ birth of a child
- ▲ death of a parent
- ▲ living in a marriage
- ▲ single experience
- ▲ looking for a new pet
- ▲ survival in school
- ▲ raising children
- ▲ reaching for a new goal

Following God into the Future

- ▲ separation from a spouse
- ▲ retirement

9. Read a letter from a friend

Read and discuss this excerpt from a letter.

Dear Ralph,

...I want to express my own commitment to change and to life. One can hold on to something like creativity, or life-affirmation, or a dynamic God to meet the challenges of change. I do not feel that "being adrift" is a fearful state, but trust this vast stream of desires and too-long channeled motivations to carry me to a far place...downstream, off to the side, up a different river, to a new body of water, to a stormy sea. Whatever, wherever! I am not afraid of its consequences.

I am appealing to my friends for support, understanding, stability. I may find all of these. I may not. Still, I have creativity, life, God.

Hey, good buddy, I'm holding together. Don't worry, but do respond.

Love, Joe

The letter was written during a time of unprecedented change in Joe's life. Does he seem up or down? Is he coping? How? Which of his affirmations strikes you as most hopeful? What advice would you like to offer Joe? What would you encourage Ralph to say to Joe? How does the attitude of the letter speak to you?

10. Make decisions

Life-prolonging (and enhancement) procedures developed in modern medicine raise critical issues about the future—issues profoundly personal and social. The possible extension of life raises an issue of personal decision making. One may write a living will or be asked to sign a similar statement upon entrance into a hospital as a patient. Questions of one's ability to make decisions about the future raise a most important issue regarding quality of life. When is a life worth living? Who makes the decision? Who should? What about when one can no longer make any decisions? What kind of future will we create?

All of these possibilities are ours due both to changing technological/medical procedures and changing public policy related to such issues. How can we be meaningfully involved in the necessary debate and truth seeking that will make our lives most meaningful, give us responsible personal power, and serve the common good? What are some new questions we should be asking?

11. Read together a biblical poem of hope 🗝

Where in Isaiah 64:1–8 are the phrases regarding the future? What are some implied changes needing to be made? Write on newsprint or marker board the sounds, smells, sensations, tastes, colors, and the like you notice in this text.

12. A bidding prayer 🗝

Gracious and eternal God, you hear us when we speak...you hear us when we are silent. Give attention to our concerns and our prayers for the future:

▲ We pray for those things that will end in our lives. *(pause)*

▲ We pray for discernment of the most important spiritual conflicts in our lives. *(pause)*

▲ We pray for the helpful insights we gathered in this study. *(pause)*

▲ We pray for understanding of the educational issues we are ready to engage. *(pause)*

Reflect on and discuss questions related to new possibilities for the extension of life.

CONNECTING WITH GOD

In a bidding prayer the leader pauses after each bid so those praying may reflect, either silently or aloud.

▲ We pray for all those changes that have redefined us as individuals and as this group. *(pause)*

▲ O God, help us to know what each of us wants for ourselves, for the church, for our community. *(pause)*

▲ Encourage us to make a commitment to one another, to our young people, to the future, and to you, O God. *(pause)*

In the name of Christ we offer our prayer. Amen.

13. Sing a song

Sing (or read the words to) "Have Thine Own Way, Lord" (*Chalice Hymnal,* no. 588 or *Hymnbook for Christian Worship*, no. 227).

14. Make survival decisions

List survival needs individually or as a group.

Think about how to survive in the light of unrelenting change. What needs to be on an adequate survival list? what tools? what processes? Make a list. Perhaps challenge group members to actually make a survival kit before the next session. List things in our experience that are already preparing us (what we know, skills acquired, decisions already made). Survive and thrive. Explore helpful God images. How can my conservatism and focus on the past work for me? How can my liberality and future orientation help? How can our group commitments move us into God's future? How does the affirmation that we move into God's future empower us? (An option might be to make a survival kit containing empty medicine bottles, slips of paper, small boxes, and the like.)

ENRICHING THE EXPERIENCE

Go to the movies

Explore views of the future in movies. As a group, see one or more of the following (at a cinema or with a video rental).

▲ *Blade Runner* (1982) Harrison Ford, Rutger Hauer, Daryl Hannah. Technology. What does it mean to be human? Very obvious theological themes. Very dark. Very brooding.

▲ *Star Trek: The Motion Picture* (1979) William Shatner, Leonard Nimoy. Similar themes to "Blade Runner" but much, much more optimistic.

▲ *Logan's Run* (1976) Michael York, Farrah Fawcett. Discrimination and oppression.

▲ *Soylent Green* (1973) Charlton Heston, Chuck Connors, Joseph Cotton. Humanity's destruction of the ecology.

▲ *Mad Max* (1979) Mel Gibson. World out of control, lawlessness, world after nuclear war.

▲ *Planet of the Apes* (1968) Charlton Heston, Roddy McDowall. What is a human/beast? World after nuclear war.

▲ *Arika* (1988) Japanese animation. Genetic engineering. Creating a master race.

▲ *Fahrenheit 451* (1966) Oskar Werner, Julie Christie.

▲ *1984* (1984) John Hurt, Richard Burton.

You may wish to review some television series. Many of the movies above were made into television series. Two good ones are

▲ *Star Trek: The Next Generation* (1987–1994).

▲ *Babylon 5* (1993–current) Bruce Boxleitner.

Have fun viewing and discussing ideas of the future. How do we make or prevent such a future as is depicted?

A movie discussion guide

If your group likes movie discussions, consider using some of these ideas to structure the talks.

1. Responses
    - What emotions did you experience in yourself?
    - What emotions did you observe in the characters?

- Which character(s) did you identify with the most?
- What was the overall mood of the picture?
2. Art observations
    - What made your favorite scene work as a scene?
    - What minor character had the most pivotal role?
    - What were the most significant lines of dialogue?
    - What did you notice about music, lighting, camera work, and so on?
3. Interpretation
    - What were the time issues involved in the movie?
    - What changes were taking place in the characters?
    - What issues of community were explored?
    - How were God or religion interpreted?
    - What were the main symbols?
    - What values were upheld?

Surf the Net

Ask for volunteers to search the Net for millennium-related activities, comments, and news. Copy some of the most interesting and pass them around the group. Use one or more as the basis for a discussion. You may want to provide a variety of resources, ranging from fundamentalist assertions of the end of the world to reports on Britain's Committee on the Millennium. Other topics you may wish to surf for class resources are *change, survival in the future, biomedical ethics,* and *science fiction.*

A future food fest

Schedule a group gathering, actually a dinner event, at a time other than the group study time. Invite the immediate families of group members or anyone the group decides on. Anyone who wishes plans, creates, and prepares a food dish that might be common, popular, or unique in some future time agreed upon by the group (e.g., 2020, 2100). The food could be of any type (e.g., gourmet, fast-food, deli, dessert, main course, appetizer, European, Mediterranean, South Pacific, Latin, African American, Native American, North American, Asian, a holiday favorite [Christmas, Valentines Day, etc.]). "Dress up" or "dress down" the food dishes. Make it imaginative, but also edible! During or after the dinner event, everyone could even vote on "names" for the dishes brought.

ABOUT FAITH CROSSINGS

"I searched for you, and searched for you, until you found me."
—Augustine, an early Christian theologian, in a prayer to God

Faith is not a static condition, something that keeps us tied down to a certain outlook. Instead, it is a companion on a journey, a great search for God. We discover that the God we search for is the God who is with us as we travel through the years of our lives.

For the Christian, faith crossings are not taken alone, not even alone with God. Ours is a faith born in community. We learn and grow from one another. Our guide on our faith travels, Jesus Christ, points out that loving God and loving our neighbor cannot be separated from one another. We need each other for support and guidance along life's road.

Faith in the God of Jesus Christ sometimes lifts us to another, spiritual realm. More often, it helps us see God's presence in the ordinary. Joseph F. Schmidt reminds us of this in his book *Praying Our Experiences* (St. Mary's Press, 1980, pp. 52–53).

> An experience of beauty or joy or a moment of intimacy may also put us in touch with an awareness of God's love and blessing. We ride on a mountain road, or walk along a beach, or experience the affection and complete acceptance of a friend, and we suddenly awake to the realization that at work in our life is a force of love and care that fully encompasses us and all of reality. We see more clearly that we are loved quite undeservedly not just by a friend but by Life. We become more aware that we and all creation are being sustained and nourished by a beneficent free Love. And in this we realize God's word uttered in blessing and care.

As we travel together in faith, we learn what love is all about. FAITH CROSSINGS, a series of small group resources, is designed to bring adult Christians together for:

▲ mutual growth in faith, love, and knowledge,

▲ mutual support and fellowship, and

▲ deepening relationship with God, Christ, and the church,

So that they may

▲ connect the Christian faith with their everyday lives and

▲ live lives of active discipleship and faithful witness.

RESOURCES

This annotated listing offers additional study and reference resources for *Following God into the Future.*

The Second Coming of the Church—A Revolutionary Model for the 21st Century, by George Barna, Word, 1997. A leading expert on church growth proposes a new way to make the church relevant again in our modern world.

Surprises by the River —The Prophecy of Ezekiel, by Jon L. Berquist, Chalice Press, 1993. This insightful study explores the scripture in terms of its themes.

At the Edges of Life—A Holistic Vision of the Human Adventure, by Bruce G. Epperly, Chalice Press, 1992. Using a combination of traditional Christian images, New Age spirituality, holistic healing, and ecological awareness, this book points the way to a vibrant new view of life and death.

In Defense of Doubt—An Invitation to Adventure, by Val Webb, Chalice Press, 1995. By exercising creative, courageous doubt, we can throw out our old, outgrown dogmas and replace them with better, more personal systems.

Dealing with Change—LifeSearch, by Bonnie Messer, Abingdon Press, 1996. A study on change and how to cope with it.

Growing Together—Understanding and Nurturing Your Child's Faith Journey, by Anne N. Rupp, Faith and Life Press, 1996. How to undertake the journey of transmitting faith and values to children.

Transforming Congregations for the Future, by Loren B. Mead, Alban Institute. Presentation on how we reshape our congregations to meet the needs of the next century.

The Bible Code, by Michael Drosnin, Simon & Schuster, 1997. The fascinating, alluring book on discerning prophecies and events forcasting from a numeric code system discovered within the text of the Bible.

LOOK FOR THESE FAITH CROSSINGS TITLES:

Available now:

God's Ordinary People—A look at some fascinating but little-known biblical characters.

Faith Talk—An introduction to basic Christian beliefs.

Following God into the Future—As we welcome a new millennium, where will our faith journeys take us?

Available December 1998:

Through the Fire—A Bible study on facing tough times.

ABC's of the Bible—Twenty-six key verses draw us into the fascinating world of the scripture.

Show No Partiality—A lively dialogue on facing the challenge of racism.

Available June 1999:

Living Water—Take the plunge—explore the rich symbolism of water in the Bible!

Worship—the Whys, Whats, and Hows—Explore vital questions about what it means to worship God.

When Christ and Caesar Meet—Never discuss religion and politics? This course takes on both!

And even more fascinating FAITH CROSSINGS courses are in the works!

To Order: Call Christian Board at 1-800-366-3383.
Visit our Web site: www.cbp21.com